Are You Listening?

First published 2020 by The Hedgehog Poetry Press

Published in the UK by
The Hedgehog Poetry Press
5, Coppack House
Churchill Avenue
Clevedon
BS21 6QW

www.hedgehogpress.co.uk

ISBN: 978-1-913499-20-4

9 8 7 6 5 4 3 2 1

A CIP Catalogue record for this book is available from the British Library.

Are You Listening?

by

Gill McEvoy

Contents

Clean Break.. 11

Stolen 12

Hands 13

Out under the Moon 14

The Wayward Button... 15

And Then.. 16

The Lonely Dead... 17

They Say the Last Colour We See is Blue 18

Derek Jarman's Film "Blue" 19

Night of the Shooting Stars, Normandy......................... 20

Stars 21

Sponsoring a Fruit Tree in Your Name........................... 22

The Bardsey Apple Tree, *eifel ynys enlli* 23

Apple Harvest 24

Now I see you, now I don't 25

Walking to the Rural Station 26

Walking at Twilight... 27

Bird-Watcher at a Window... 28

Glass Bird in a Shop Window... 29

Dunlin on the Estuary.. 30

In Red and White 31

October 32

Bedsit, Herbert Place, Dublin 33

Wilton Place, Dublin, 1969 34

Small Boy Walking past Belsen Corpses 35

Hooked by my Sash 36

First Dinner Date 37

St Valentine's Day 38

Colour 39

The Way You 40

Spear Thistle 41

The Whippoorwill 42

Tobacco Harvest, North Carolina 43

Bearings 44

Peaches for Pickling 45

Atlantic Coast, S. Carolina 46

Spring Flowers on the Highway Verge, Texas 47

The Luxury of Sleep 48

The Night Train Whistles Through Smithville 49

Locked Away 50

As If 51

Finish 52

There 53

Here 54

The Nettle Coat 55

Masquerade...56

The Gravedigger 57

On the Staircase in the National Gallery.......................................58

A God Day..59

Wallowing 60

Growth Rings..61

The Wrong Side of the Holly Bush..62

In December..63

Old Wounds 64

Privilege 65

For You 66

When God Made Time 67

Acknowledgements: 70

This collection traces the story of a grief which, as P.D. James said of her own grief, instead of diminishing, grew more intense with the passing of time.

CLEAN BREAK

The last sound you made was the thud
of your coffin hitting earth.

After that solemn thump the spatter
of soil on the lid was like
the itch of plaster on the skin
after the leg is set.

The break was clean.

STOLEN

All night I sat with you
until the dawn was coming up.

I leaned against the window wall –
how cold that felt and yet
the ward so hot.

A horse and rider came in view,
high-stepping on the road,

(the sealed glass too thick
to let me hear
the strike of metal shoe on stone).

Gloved together
horse and rider moved as one.

When I asked about this later
the nurses eyed me strangely,
shook their heads -

No, no horse, no rider.

But I saw. I saw them.

In that wide and empty dawn
they came for you.

HANDS

All those months I nursed you,
coming, going, busy in your room
taking soiled clothes away,
bringing food you wouldn't eat
or upset in a rage across the floor.

I washed and dressed you.
Sometimes
I'd press my hand against your skin
in sorrow and in love.

You're washed and dressed now
for the last time.
I take your hand in mine,
tell you how I love you.

But your hands no longer move.

OUT UNDER THE MOON

The bald light
of this winter moon
paints the trees
and roofs black.

Its cold eye has no use for greys
or in-betweens;
it has no will to soften edges.

The night is sharp in black
and silver.

Bleak
as the coldness of a moon
which feels nothing.

THE WAYWARD BUTTON

I burnt your coat in November,
Bonfire Night, when else?
God knows that coat was you,
stubborn in the way it wouldn't burn,
awkward in the way it slumped on top the pile,
out of shape with everything,
the world, itself.

That coat was every morning
when I couldn't start the day on time;
you to wash and dress, kids to get to school,
and you, soiled again; three more lines
of washing, sheets, pyjamas, towels,
to hang outside.

That coat was each Day Centre afternoon
when you refused to get in the car and I,
with murder in my heart – shopping to fetch,
washing to bring in before the rain,
dinner burning slowly on the stove –
would force you in, all sixteen stone,
then feel the scald of tears.

It played a last trick when it burned;
a button loosed by flame fell from the fire,
rolled to rest at my right foot. It lay there
like a small dog begging amnesty.
Next morning when I raked the ashes flat
I picked it up. Now it goes
everywhere with me.

AND THEN

A missal. A rosary of jet,
its metal links tarnished as if
you'd never used it much.

A brown wool coat
whose shape was your shape,
bent and out of skew.

One button missing.
Like you.

THE LONELY DEAD

They die alone and no-one notices until
the stench is forced out underneath the sill.
Police or Council come, break down the door,
take the rotted corpse away.
Then someone has to clean the place,
rip out the filthy carpets, clear the flies
and maggots, hurl the foetid rubbish into skips,
bag up the sad misshapen shoes,
the clothes, old letters, last year's news:
the shock of someone else's life: dried flowers
kept in tissue, sugar cubes collected from abroad,
a child's toy, a bag of defunct coins,
kept perhaps to pay death's ferry-man:
all the tender waste to break the heart,
as if the dead still speak; as if they can.

THEY SAY THE LAST COLOUR WE SEE IS BLUE

Before the light went
what did you think of?

Indigo, cerulean,
cobalt, marine, navy,
the artist's catalogue of blues?

African skies,
the clear blue cross on the Finnish flag,
purple-blue of Irish hills,

the blue of Gougane Barra's lake?

Or the perfect blue
of the small forget-me-not,

its yellow eye a tiny sun,
its name a plea?

DEREK JARMAN'S FILM "BLUE"

His silence now is blue. As if an artist drew
a laden brush of paint from alder buds to reeds,
his mind and mouth and tongue are flushed
by blue: the low-slung sky, the feathered seeds,

the brook like navy slate beneath a moon,
the tassels of phalaris plumes fused
with the moody amethyst of alder buds;
blue dancing in the rain-logged field's flood,

and blue the cold stars whirling in his head.
He knows that in this moment as he speaks
"cyan, cobalt, indigo" will float
like moulted feathers from his throat,

his tongue become the painter's brush
that coats the world in this deep blue hush.

NIGHT OF THE SHOOTING STARS, NORMANDY

Along the beaches phosphorus
flashed green and blue
as every rush of tide
breached the sea-weed barricades.

We lay on our backs to watch
the stars that burst like mortars
then fell into the night.

Later, sand abrading our skin,
the bed-sheets grainy as rust,
we licked salt
from each other's lips.

It was hot and sharp
on our tongues,
like cordite.

STARS

You could name them.
I could not.
Look! There's Cassiopeia!

I couldn't find it till you said
It's like a W,
stood back
to point it out to me

and fell.

That was the moment
all the stars went out.

SPONSORING A FRUIT TREE IN YOUR NAME...

I have not placed a stone for you
and nothing marks your grave
but creeping cinquefoil and grass.

Apples did not grow in Cork,
not in orchards, not in rows.

The tree-rows here are neatly made
by equidistance, harmonies –

I'm not sure that you'd like to be
included in their ranks
(chaotic as you were)

yet I like the thought of you transformed
to apple, greengage, plum or pear.

THE BARDSEY APPLE TREE, *EIFEL YNYS ENLLI*

The air is apple, seaweed,
loud with the bark of seals,
gull shrieks,
the redshank's trill.

Orchard of one,
the apple-tree clutches the wall
of this house, sheltering from
the scorch and blast of storms.

Blossom is brief,
torn away by wind
before the bees are out.

In the autumn gales
the apples mummify,
dried by wind and salt.

APPLE HARVEST

Apples cobble the orchard floor.
At my feet the zebra'd gold of wasps.
The basket on my hip is full.

I rest it on the wooden table
left out underneath these trees,
its grain split like the bursting fruit.

The bones of the basket are brittle.
The trees are cragged and bowed.
But still each year the wasps come,

lurching from the apples into flight,
staggering upwards in the air.

NOW I SEE YOU, NOW I DON'T

Since you died
you pop up in the oddest spots –
there by a lamp in an unknown street
when I'm looking for a space to park,
or disappearing down a summer lane
on a bicycle perhaps, or on a horse.

You lurk in someone else's face,
you hide in other people's skin,
a gesture here, a movement of the hand,
the head. I turn: it's you, it's you!
then it isn't anyone I know
and you are gone again.

WALKING TO THE RURAL STATION

In this cottage someone's playing a recorder.
The notes fly, one by one, into the thatch.

A heron flaps up from the pond-edge,
voicing its objection.

A gasp of breeze shuffles the leaves.
It might rain.

The train to Newport is always late.
The hills are blue with waiting.

For days this friend has not known
what to do with herself.

She should take a train to somewhere.

Anywhere.

WALKING AT TWILIGHT

At this hour the sky's blue
deepens like thought.

An owl calls, a tawny,
calling to its mate.

Terwhit, the cry rings
through the dark branches.

Far off, an answer comes:
Terwhoo, terwhoo;

Talking back to you.
Talking back.

BIRD-WATCHER AT A WINDOW

Too windy today for birds,
he studies the blown clouds.

A glance of light has flared perhaps
from the polished lens –

below, a woman walking with a dog
glares up at the same moment
he looks down

to meet her outraged face
caught in the circle
of his glass.

The full clouds start to moult
fine quills of rain;

she puts her head down,
hauls her dog behind her,
storming off.

He lays his binoculars
aside, feeling illogically
ashamed.

GLASS BIRD IN A SHOP WINDOW

Surely the maker of this bird is
one whose winter months are lived
among deep silences of snow,

who understands the blue and purple
bruise of folds among the drifts,
who knows

the strange transparencies of ice,
the way light toes on it
a fragile dance?

I have been standing here so long
my feet have slipped into
boots of fur,

snow is settling on my shoulders
under dank green pine
and snow-locked birch.

Ice splits; a bird flies up,
freckles the freezing air
with blue.

A shudder of snow
ushers its escape.

DUNLIN ON THE ESTUARY

Water sucking backwards over mud
tide on the ebb

ladder of wings
shuttles up

black cloud of birds

carves
up the estuary

whirring
like some terrible machine

its shadow moving
under it.

IN RED AND WHITE

You could helter-skelter down their columns on a rug or tray,
pretend they're giant sticks of rock in red and white –

slice through their middles and you'd surely find
the names of places where they stand:
Strumble, Needles, Bardsey, Portland Bill.

In the wind you'd hear the thin bewildered sighs
of long-forgotten keepers drifting round
the eerie robot systems that transmit the beams;

men amazed that no-one has to trim or light the lamps.

OCTOBER

Fourteen was the number of the bus
that took me to St Cloud,
the house at number fourteen in the square,
a Georgian house turned into flats -
fourteen occupants lived there.

Three students on the first floor- that was us;
three nurses on the ground;
St Cloud, at fourteen in the square,
"topped and tailed" by eight young men,
buzzed with come-and-go, the callings there.

Three times fourteen years have passed;
I walk and watch the falling leaves,
wish it were *that* October now -
in a house that hummed like a hive of bees.

BEDSIT, HERBERT PLACE, DUBLIN

Each night we let down the hard mattress
of the bed-settee, unrolled our blankets,
crawled into sleep that was fractured
by the crash and curse of Dublin on the prowl,
the cars that nightly cruised by the canal.

Though we knew what went on at the front,
the shady low-life acting out its script
beside the water under trees,

we slept at last
like two white poppies in the dark,
closed and innocent.

WILTON PLACE, DUBLIN, 1969

(For Derek Mahon)

Every bit the country gentleman back then.
Tweed jacket, twill trousers.

Shoes well polished.
Courteous manners.

And quiet,
so quiet he never said much about himself,
only about poetry or possibly a student.

We sat at break with our cups of tea
in a room panelled in wood.

Had there been a green-shaded lamp,
a mahogany desk and a leather chair
it would have suited him well.

As would a pipe on which to suck
while he reflected.

Tea-break ended, his reflections
were never voiced.
He was probably always thinking

as he sat there with his cooling mug,
of that fungal shed in County Wexford,
the lost people of Treblinka.

SMALL BOY WALKING PAST BELSEN CORPSES

(from the war photographs of George Rodger)

They're stretched on the verges,
ribs like the teeth of combs,
skull plates pushing through
shrunken layers of skin.

So many. So many.

The boy is thinking of a game of marbles,
his pockets full of them.

Marbles.

Like so many glazed eyes.

HOOKED BY MY SASH

Three a.m. Silk sweeps my skin
like a lover's exploring hand.

We spin and whirl, not wanting
the night of the Ball to end,
you in your coat tails, I in my heels,
under the crescent moon.

My dress thrills
to the wind's sudden stir,
fills like a parachute,
snatches me up.

Its sash hooks over
the moon's thin horn,
leaves me dangling under the stars,
watching your face grow small.

FIRST DINNER DATE

Slubbed silk it was, my dress,
with small green scallops
round the neck, like leaves.
Too tight round the hips.

Was it wanting you so much
or just the dress that hurt?

For I could only breathe
in shallow spaces of my lungs
as if the restaurant
were sited on a mountain top.

ST VALENTINE'S DAY

This is our wedding day
and overnight in this sleepless city,
Dublin, it has snowed.

Today the world is whiter
than the dress that hangs
beside my bed in readiness.

Beyond ice-patterned glass
the garden wears
a wedding veil of snow.

I race outside to make my mark,
pressing my bare feet down
as if I could print this day

somehow upon Eternity –
delight and snow.

COLOUR

You understood what it was to see
colour others said weren't there.

I said the pines were violet
in the navy light

And you would squeeze your lids together,
and say it could be so.

THE WAY YOU

It was the way you seemed to bounce
across Front Square as if your body held
some inner joy; the way you wouldn't dance
at parties but sat there, pipe in mouth,
considering the quainter follies
of the human race.

The way, later, you referred to me always
as "*my* wife", not "*the* wife"
as some men do.

It was all of these.
And I wanted it to last
forever.

SPEAR THISTLE

Silver threaded through its spikes
like sheep-wool on barbed wire,

each head enough
for a thousand crowns of thorn.

THE WHIPPOORWILL

Beyond the fields of bluets,
beyond the red oaks
cloaked in vines
of scuppernong
he calls his drawn-out cry of
whip-poor-will, whip-poor-will.

His cry brings out the stars.

Their icy distance shrinks away
the humid, clammy Carolina day.

TOBACCO HARVEST, NORTH CAROLINA

All afternoon we laboured bunching leaves.
Black ooze glued our fingers to our thighs
each time we wiped our hands off on our jeans.

'Tobacco cu'in' sheds': the foreman flung
the barn-doors open to a brimstone stink
of bunches hung in twos, like pairs of lungs.

The bright greens slowly grieve their way to rust.
'Killin' sheds' I muttered to myself,
examining my hands – thick tar and dust.

BEARINGS

Fireflies fill the night
with sparks,

flicker, flare,
like faulty electricity.

I feel for the sandy track
with naked feet.

Pines and hickories have blocked out
all the light.

The chill lake shocks me
into gasp

as I wade waist-deep,
stop to get my bearings.

In the round gap the trees
have left

so many stars
the night can't breathe;

the water's mirror staggered
by their weight.

I'm swept round in
a dizzy spin of stars,
a carousel of fireflies.

PEACHES FOR PICKLING

They are wedged in their bushel basket
like a crowd in stadium
cheering the sun's ball on its arc
from rise to fall, their ripe scent
surging like a chant of summer.

She spills them out on the tabletop.
They scurry, scatter, hesitate
then shiver to a stop
as if they were oddly cold inside
their felted skins of fur.

How will it be tonight,
her knives and pickling pans all done,
each fruit bald and naked
in the mirror
of the jars?

ATLANTIC COAST, S. CAROLINA

The speech slow and sweet as treacle,
pale skeins of Spanish moss softening the trees,
even the crabs have soft shells,
are eaten whole.

Long history of night riders in white sheets,
slave-drivers in the cotton fields.

Under the soft shells
whips and knives.

SPRING FLOWERS ON THE HIGHWAY VERGE, TEXAS

We were quick to learn to name these flowers –
Indian paintbrush, prickly poppy, winecups,
bluebonnets everywhere like sheets of sky.

Bees head-down at endless desks of pollen,
butterflies more brilliant than the flowers themselves,
katydids, a hornet dancing underneath the trees.

But that caterpillar, black and green on the eerie
green and white of poisonous asclepiad
made us see that really we knew nothing –

not which creatures lived on what, nor how
they interlinked, and certainly not the kind
of butterfly the caterpillar would become.

We were as blank as all those drivers hurrying
up the highway who stared at us where we stood,
propping up our too-big bicycles, heads down

in prickly poppies, lilies, winecups.

THE LUXURY OF SLEEP

Under the burning morning sun,
in N.C's close and humid heat
we would dig and rake and sow,
planting lettuce, corn and black-eyed peas
(we never knew what to do with these
but grew them anyway).

After an hour your fair skin
could take no more and you'd retreat
to the shade of dog-wood and the pines,
resting your back against a trunk, a can
of thin American beer in your hand
while I, who loved the heat, worked on.

Later, exhausted by the work and sun,
I'd lie down in the afternoon
in the semi-darkness of our room.
You would join me, hold me close,
and I would sleep.

On nights when the dark seems endless
and the hours slow, it taunts me now,
that sleep back then, animal, comfortable,
deep, so deep.

THE NIGHT TRAIN WHISTLES THROUGH SMITHVILLE

with no full-stop to bullfrogs booming by the lake,
no interruption of cicada's churr and slur but I
am snatched from sleep with anguish in my soul.

Haunted by its lonely banshee cry
I rise and ghost across the midnight grass,
my feet pulled to its urgency of sound.

I could jump a box-car, ride this train
through the huge bowl of this southern night,
past redwood, pinewood forests, gorges,

mountains, snow, red deserts, to some great city,
a dozen states away from here. All that.

How damp my cheeks are when I climb back into bed.

LOCKED AWAY

Last night cloud came down like a weight
of feathers, whited out our little house.

I wheel you out to say good morning to the day;
you waggle useless hands as though to part the mist

that curtains you from me. Soft as heartbeats I can hear
the steady weep of wet from vanished trees.

The world is locked away: no insects, birds.
Their absence haunts the day

Our breath snags on the milky air
like words we'll never say.

I push the body-shell from which the *you* has gone
and ask myself, how long can this go on?

AS IF

As if we'd just turned the light off,
and silence had fallen,
you having had the last word.

As if any moment you might
rise, step into the dark garden
polishing the lens of your telescope
as you set it up;

as if the night-sky could cast again its magic,
we two counting constellations,
watching for shooting stars,

As if morticians were not so skilled
that they have you lying there
looking so alive
you might suddenly speak.

As if it is possible to find the brightness
in the stars again.

FINISH

It ends.

Over.

Done.

Everything ends.

End of everything.

I move.

Away.

Away.

THERE

where trees crept up to the cottage walls at night,
where, hidden in shrubs, the young stag
raised his velvet branches to the dawn
where the owl sat brooding on his bough
in autumn mist that swallowed up the day,
where the primrose lit the paths of spring
and bluebells trembled underneath the moon,
where our window was a triangle of trees and sunrise,
where the Rayburn glowed and the huge oak table
filled the room, where books padded the width and breadth
of every rough stone wall, where the curtains
were printed with huge blue plums, green pears,
red apples, their names in bold in French,
prune, poire, pomme.
There.
Where someone else lives now.

HERE

You would have liked it here.

There are trees, there is rain,
the neighbours are friendly.

The light in the rooms is green.

Green, like your eyes
that glinted a sea-change
whenever a story rose in your mind.

Your green eyes are closed now
and I do not imagine you still telling stories
in some other country of trees and rain.

The light in this house is green.

I wish you could know.

THE NETTLE COAT

(a design by artist Alice Maher)

It has lost its vegetable stink
of raw and turnipy seepage
long ago,

the drying of the nettles saw to that.

The dead leaves do not pins-and-needle you
with burning sting each time you touch.

And nettles, dried, are strong as rope.

Yet no-one wants to hug me
in my handsome nettle coat.

MASQUERADE

Let loose by sun on bevelled glass,
a circus of sequins
parades into my room:

troupes of clowns with pots of paint
spatter the shadows with rainbows,
back-flip on the walls, daub the cupboard
with reds and orange,
splatter the fridge in green and purple silks,
cover the dog in blue and violet spots.

Spider tightropes spin out tinselled threads,
strings of dancing horses shake
their plumes of gold and green and indigo,
colour capers on my arms and hands.

The sun moves on beyond the window,
the masquerade departs.

The cupboard resumes its dark sobriety,
shadows are shadows once again.

Only the fridge continues humming to itself,
remembering something quite remarkable.

THE GRAVEDIGGER

He leans his elbows on the straight-cut sides,
tells me he used a ladder when he first began –
Who would fancy being stuck down here? he grins,
Now, he says, he jumps – and shows me how,
touching his palms to the sore earth, springing out.

He's sun-baked like old pots, says that's what
he often finds down here - fragments mostly.
He takes a flask of tea and offers me.
I shake my head. He perches on a tombstone,
motions me to do the same. I refuse again.

He laughs. *They'll never know, poor sods.*
What matters is the living. The dead
are solid weights and it can be a nasty shock,
that thud, so me, I line my graves. Always.
Long grass is best,

especially after heavy rains – no-one wants
to hear that splash, that can really set them off,
so I line it good and thick, the box
will drop more gently then.

Later I think of all he said, imagine
lying for all eternity in the long grass,
almost envy the dead their luck.

ON THE STAIRCASE IN THE NATIONAL GALLERY

She seized immediate possession of the stairs
though there was room for all.

small fierce Moses of light, she billowed past,
descending like a tiny hurricane
in her long green coat and yellow boots.

We parted like the Red Sea waves,
fell back, dazed, as if the Book
of Revelations had opened on the stairs,

let loose a sudden angel of fire
who swept past in a roaring heat of wind.

After a while the air regained its calm.
We continued up, for nothing
really had happened there;

but each of us looked privately
for the scorch of flame on every stair.

A GOD DAY

(We used to say a good day was a day
given us by God)

It's a God day
when orange tips and holly blues
flicker in the hedgerows,

a God day
when the sky holds over you
an arc of purest blue,

a God day
when you walk in yellow fields of rape,
plunge into the heart of the sun.

WALLOWING

She is out in rain that clings
to the wool of sheep like a halo of light,
rain the Irish call *soft.*

The days of dry, dead weather are over.

Now she may fill the bath to the brim
and wallow,
soak her garden till the roses sigh.

GROWTH RINGS

Once I was willow, my narrow skirt
a strip of sunlight in the woodland,
my blouse an unfurled leaf.

As maple I wore skirts of scarlet,
fretted sleeves
that showed my skin like clouds.

Now oak.
Jackets of knubble and gnarl.
Thickening, thickening.

Acorns at my feet.

THE WRONG SIDE OF THE HOLLY BUSH

It was too steep for us and so we slid.
At the bottom we saw that the path
we used to know so well
was on the other side of the bush -
the easier path, less steep.

But that was then,
when our children were young,
our husbands still alive.

Like a sudden hammer blow falling,
it occurs to us that we are not
on the wrong side
of the holly bush at all,

simply on the *other* side

where the paths are different now.

IN DECEMBER

In this month each year
I visit you,

crossing the water that divides us
till my feet touch land.

I come to you now with flowers,
lay them on your quilt of grass.

In the private silence of this cemetery
I tell you everything.

OLD WOUNDS

'Because of your love', you wrote me once,
quoting from a poem I didn't know,
'there is gold in the depths of my dreams'.
Where are those dreams now? By chance,

polished by all the years I clutched it tight,
time left me one small thing, a stone,
of all those simple gifts you brought:
a beetle's wing that glowed with burnished light,

a leaf, a fragile bird-bone, natural things that I
delighted in. *Time*, they say, *will heal.* I say no:
wounds and bruises deepen. In my sleep
they burrow in and sharply let me know

that love is made of grief and hurt, and lasts beyond
the point at which, you think, you'd let it go.

PRIVILEGE

I follow the sun from room to room
in a house where only a dog and
my shadow haunt my steps.

The fall of sunlight in this house
is kind, a hand stretched out
to heal a wound.

Light, my guardian in a house
where the light that falls
into the rooms
is green.

FOR YOU

Tonight the stars are like apples
crowding the tree.
You could have picked them one by one,
kept them in the pocket
closest to your heart.

But it is I who watch the stars,
I who cannot name them as you did.
The pockets of my heart are filled
with holes, not stars, the bright apples
always out of reach.

WHEN GOD MADE TIME

I used to hate that phrase ,
that *by the way* of yours
which meant we'd be the last to leave

Our hosts dancing on their toes,
hands on the doorknob,
smiling through their teeth...

but your stories were so good.

Turn right, I'd say, navigating as you drove,
and you'd turn left
as if you couldn't bear to follow orders.

Only you could take an hour
to go three miles,
using one of your 'infallible' short cuts.

I came to know that beech knoll
on the top of Frankby hill so well:
once, twice, *three* times around.

I gave you a watch; still you were always late:

When God *made time he made plenty of it,*
you joked.

I'm the one left with all that time.

And I forgive you everything.

ACKNOWLEDGEMENTS:

My thanks to the editors of the following magazines in which some of these poems were first published:

Agenda, The Interpreter's House, Acumen, Under the Radar, The High Window, Envoi, The Frogmore Papers, South, Stand, The Journal, Atrium, The Stony Thursday Book, Crannog, Haverthorn, Ink Sweat and Tears, The Lonely Crowd, Other Poetry, And Other Poems, Dream Catcher, Artemis, Iota, The Cannon's Mouth, The Ugly Tree, Poetry Scotland.

Thanks also to the organisers of the following competitions:

The English Fellows' Association Poetry Prize, 2009 and 2010
Poetry on the Lake
The Enfield Prize
Eastern Light
Flamingo Feathers Competition

And to the editors of the following anthologies:

The Darker Side of Love (Paper Swans Press)
The Book of Love and Loss (ed R V Bailey and June Hall)
Ten Poems about Snow (Candlestick Press)

Versions of some of these poems were previously published in "Uncertain Days" (Happenstance Press 2006), and "The Plucking Shed" (Cinnamon Press, 2010)

Lightning Source UK Ltd.
Milton Keynes UK
UKHW012352150121
377117UK00001B/5